Joy Ride

Ron Slate

T0025858

Carnegie Mellon University Press
Pittsburgh 2023

Acknowledgments

I wish to thank the editors of the following publications in which these poems or versions of them first appeared:

The American Poetry Review: "A Vigil"
Guesthouse: "He Decided to Go to Kuzguncuk"
Literary Matters: "Tbilisi / Baku" and "Brother / ICU"
Plume and *Plume Anthology*: "Naked City," "From a Line by Kawabata," "The Dangers of Contemplation," "Between the Bed and the Window," "'What Is This Thing Called Love?'" and "Stop-Time"
Scoundrel Time: "The Work"
Poetry London: "At Sardent"
The Volta: "Joy Ride"

"Night Crossing" originally appeared in Poem-a-Day (Academy of American Poets).

"Joy Ride" was also published in the anthology *More Truly and More Strange: 100 Contemporary American Self-Portrait Poems* (Persea Books 2020), edited by Lisa Russ Spaar.

I am grateful for the efforts of my friends to improve my work, and am especially indebted to Katie Peterson and Alice Fulton for their candor and collegiality. As always, Floyd Skloot's care and encouragement supported me.

Book design by Trevor Lazar

Library of Congress Control Number 2022943737
ISBN 978-0-88748-690-6
Copyright © 2023 by Ron Slate
All rights reserved
Printed and bound in the United States of America

10 9 8 7 6 5 4 3 2 1

In memory of David Clewell

"Until your heartbeat's back where it belongs
to what's alive, still going on, not gone."

Contents

I.

11 The Work
13 At Sardent
14 Brother / ICU
16 Tbilisi / Baku
19 Night Crossing
21 A Vigil
23 He Decided to Go to Kuzguncuk
25 At Sardent (II)
27 A Detail from "At Sardent (II)"
28 An Argument in the Street
29 Transit
31 After a Sudden Death
33 No-Show
35 Anniversary
37 "The Utrillo Is Lost Forever"
39 House Falling into the Sea

II.

43 Aground
45 The Dangers of Contemplation
47 Naked City
50 Ask Me Now
51 From a Line by Kawabata
53 At a Conference on the Syrian Exiles
55 Neighborhood Watch
56 Between the Bed and the Window

58   Stop-Time

60   "What Is This Thing Called Love?"

62   Dog Pacing a Balcony

63   Image of a Path Through Woods

65   Recessional

67   Boat Too Costly to Keep

69   Joy Ride

71   Notes

I.

The Work

At the dock, we loaded scallops from the boat's hold
into the truck, scraping steel on shell. All morning
we dumped bushels of them on the long tables,
until sunset we dumped gutted shells into the truck.
It was the summer after leaving the university for good.

*

In the big company, they gave us goals, roughly seasonal.
You had to account for your presence. As if when you show yourself
the hidden elements don't exist.

*

Five days a week for fifty years, my father drove the few miles
from the house to his liquor store and back.
Like a lookout on shore scanning the horizon,
he took Wednesdays off waiting for Thursday.

*

The arrival of the noon ferry, horn blasting, verified
my wages for the morning. A good shucker could open
300 shells in an hour. We lugged the full garbage cans.
At that time, the one o'clock ferry's departing horn
signified nothing to me.

*

I traveled for the big company to meet with people
forced to speak my language and follow my lead.
As entertainment, my co-workers ferried us from Hong Kong

to Macau where they lost their wages at baccarat.
On the return trip one asked, "What will you do
after your workdays have ended?"

*

Then one day after many years and jobs,
the trade I was taught, the technique I knew by heart
took me by surprise. It occurred to me that everything
in the world is raw stock for this work.
By then I was beyond the age
when most people died a hundred years ago.
You seem different, said my barber. Or maybe just older.

*

Yesterday along the roadside, I saw first-time offenders
picking up trash, protected and exposed by their orange vests.
I drove by the worksite on the way to the doctor.

*

On his deathbed, my father said he had seven regrets
but didn't name them. The accounting had agitated him for hours.
My inheritance—those who claim not to be concealed
are deceptive employees.

*

I undressed my body for the doctor. Her job is to keep me working.
She stood behind me and drew a line across my shoulder.
She said, this is how long I must make your scar.

At Sardent

I traveled to a place because something happened there or failed
to happen, my mother didn't die as a child, she wasn't carried off,
the family hid for five years though few stories are told
because so little occurred. My great-uncle Abrasha had a motorcycle
and crashed it. The present used to be a turnstile from past to future,
but now the moment is employed to say no *that* was what happened, *this*
is what's coming, millions of versions beyond grasp and control,
deleted and rewritten. I traveled to a place to watch history
vanish, the silence between the stone houses smelled like baked stone,
lily stalks were studded with corms ready for picking.
Small artichokes on erect stems—their thorns sundered my thoughts.
A tabac, gas station, church and cemetery, fountain in the middle
of the square, an old Citroën drove around it and parked
beside the cracked war memorial. *Why do you want to go there*
asked my mother. Because the past doesn't grow around us
like a grapevine. *Oh yes it does.* The newspaper in my tote bag
proved we have never moved forward, the villagers of Sardent
heard the church bell toll the late afternoon hour,
and a fourteen-wheeler hauling farm equipment rumbled
through the square. We walked down the lanes, then out toward the fields,
the dirt road and the farmhouse where the family had huddled at night.
Then back to the square and its riddled wall telling what passed
through the bodies of the executed. I stuck my fingertips
into the holes, there was a surge of excess time
swirling around the fountain. Those ancient tales of life on earth
ending forever? There's love for a world with limits.

Brother / ICU

Eventually he would come around
with a gift and indicate the value
as if he were the cause of my violence.
The voice seizes up in that instance
as the thing is flung against the wall.
In the wake of the smash, nothing can be heard,
as after a train passes an open window.
It was that familiar. Which wails the loudest,
the wall or the thing? The calm after the question.
What made him sullen made me savage.

*

The last gift was a memoir of The Great War.
A German soldier would crawl on his belly
toward the English trenches to overhear the talk.
Esteemed as a spy, he lay at the edge of exposure
for entirely different reasons.

*

For eleven days my brother lay comatose in the ICU.
I couldn't undertake the sorrows of the world.
I sat on a chair provided for the waiting and read—
*The medics tried to keep him alive on cognac
and camphor, but the needle pointed to death*

*

There was a half-light in which we once played,
halved again as my self grew imaginary.
All those years I entered and returned

through the portal, but also struggled not to enter
at all. The loyal quarter-light followed me.

*

In the waiting room, a receptionist sprinkled fish food
on the aquarium's waters . . . My brother and I crouched
at the end of the pier, each dared the other to dive.
He jumped in. I flung a stone and waited for the splash.
Years passed as he swam back to shore.
The other—still listening for the splash.

*

You've never thrown anything in anger
except that one time, she said.
At least not against a wall.

*

In those fields of filled-in trenches,
the place quivers with departed life
because one stands there almost thoughtlessly.
I crawled back as if I wanted to tell you.

Tbilisi / Baku

Our plan—a visit to the cities of our grandmothers,
Tbilisi for me, Baku for Hamid.

The voice of a Turkish pilot woke me from a dream
of a woman falling into a ditch as we walked along together.

June the fifth, the thermal springs
beneath Tbilisi fed the persimmon trees
in the hotel courtyard. In the street,
workers were felling the old plane trees
while a few protesters looked on.

At breakfast, Hamid would not relent
until I conceded there are no great French composers.

I walked to Grishashvili Street, looking
for my grandmother's birthplace, the building
where the family's clothes-making business thrived
until the Red Army shoved aside the hapless Georgian resistance.

Further along, workers were tearing down
Lermontov's house to make room for a mall,
other houses had been demolished. Hacked off heads
of griffins and pieces of cherubs lay at my feet.

I sat alone in a Kazahk restaurant
jotting the Georgian alphabet on a flyer
offering knockoff Hollywood DVDs. The waiter said
add twenty percent to the menu prices,
then stepped outside for a smoke.

The plane trees—people are allergic to them,
claimed the health ministry, and the trees are infested,
but privately they said blocking the views
of the old façades is bad for tourism.

The electricity died as I ate, the smell of sulphur
drifted in from the bathhouse next door
with the scent of fenugreek from the open market.

We took the night train to Baku.
I listened to Debussy on my headset.

June the tenth, the natural gas beneath Baku
seeping through sandstone fed the hillside fires above the city,
flames as eternal as the Zoroastrian gods.
Hamid's grandmother had prayed to them.

Everywhere, the cloying smell of crude oil, repellent
and sweet. The Old Town, filled with feral cats
and cleansed of Armenians. Posters for a Warhol show
in the ultramodern museum.

In the hotel lobby, Hamid raised his voice
to a human rights watcher from Stockholm.
They just threw the opposition leaders in jail,
Hamid said to me, it's all about money now,
you should know, you spent years
in corporations. He went up to his room.

In the morning, I found a note slipped under my door—
I love you but it is no longer a pleasure
to be with you.

I went on to Paris to visit my cousins.
As a keepsake, here is this griffin's head
carried through customs as the gendarmes
raced off in pursuit of a suspicious object.

Night Crossing

Back and forth is a way to move
when the visible is spacious.

But what's the state of the last boat,
lightly loaded and unprofitable?

Tied up at the mainland dock,
the ferry shudders in its berth,

its captain consults a tide chart
and grunts. A new, possessive moon.

Late departure, a rigid beam of light
probes the sea lane for what violates or drifts.

The other shore, not far off, can leap
and hurt the hand pointing at it.

In the dark alongside—wings seen, instantly gone,
a half thought interrupted by a heave.

Then the ferry turns hard aport to the channel,
the parting waters make the sound of a god

murmuring for both the first and last time.
At mid-crossing, something is lacking twice over—

in this location, in the mechanism or vision of the crossing.
Two ports, both accommodating, but unmoved

by what goes on between. How many departures
does a person need, how many starts can be tolerated?

A necessary collision at the pilings
tells everyone it's over.

A Vigil

Soon it was my turn to sit with my cousin's body.

They took away my navel orange and bottle of water
since to chew and swallow were acts now impossible for the body,
offensive to its state in the bardo.

The lawyers were sorting through things
in his musty apartment across town—where's the will, the accounts,
the insurance policy? He lived alone there alone for twenty-five years,
his mother's wig in a drawer, his father's hat on a hook.

He was a dentist but maintained the fiction of being
a business consultant in order to attend trade shows—
technology, textiles, furniture, candy and toys.

During the vigil, it is forbidden to fulfill a commandment,
again, to avoid insulting the limited range of the dead.

His place was stacked high with boxes of brochures,
you could smell the mildewing paper and the demise
of aging materials comprising the house.
Cartons of free samples, many items no longer for sale—
dried up ballpoints, baby foods, shoe polish.

At family events he warned us
of the rise of masses of people with grievances—
those who neither invent nor build anything,
those who bloat from food stamps spent on snack foods,
those with no feel for history or culture.
You distribute the wealth, he said, you end with Stalin.

So we were baffled to discover he practiced his dentistry
two nights a week for free in a community clinic.
If there's a man, there's a problem, said Stalin. *No man, no problem.*

The lawyers found his checkbook and tax returns.
His assets were modest. No unstamped pages in his passport.
I called him cousin but the family connection was obscure.
We were most at peace with each other when talking
about our travels, especially neglected historical sites.

He would wear a jacket and tie to dinner but he was not so groomed
and he smelled vaguely of fish. At one point during the vigil,
I nodded off, then a hand shook me roughly by the shoulder.
How many years ago did I turn my face away from him?

He Decided to Go to Kuzguncuk

A moth disappeared into the gut of a swallow that traced transparencies above everything called founded and fixed. At a point on the arc of the swoop, the moth was taken into darkness.

My grandfather took the train from Paris to visit his cousin, Maxim, in Geneva. He rarely traveled without my grandmother. The two cousins ate moussaka in a Turkish restaurant, then my grandfather said, "I'd like to see Istanbul again before I die, let's go."

Apparently this wasn't a sudden decision—he had brought a map of Istanbul with the intention of enlisting Maxim. He placed a fingertip on the neighborhood of Kuzguncuk, across the Bosphorus from the old city, at the location of the dock and a marble fountain where, as a boy, he waited for his father who would return by ferry after closing his jewelry shop for the night.

Maxim told the story years ago to Serge who finally told me via phone as I watched the swallow.

So, they went to Istanbul and walked through the district. My grandfather told Maxim, "This was my grade school run by German Lutherans, can you imagine, a boy named Abram singing choir hymns— *Oh, that I had a thousand voices to praise my God with a thousand tongues!*"

Are we truly traces of the world we trace? It was 1967, the Armenians were gone, the Greeks were gone, and the Jews. In my grandfather's youth, when a funeral procession rolled down Icadiye Street, people emerged from their houses to pay respects, no matter their messiah.

When I was a child, my grandfather would take me to the Clam Box for lunch by the beach. He would ask me about my girlfriends while gulls peered at our food from above. I would ask him about the war and his internment in the camp near Lyon, where he sometimes translated under duress for the Vichy. "Those Lutherans saved my life by teaching me German." He liked to say, "There are only three questions to ask in your life."

I thanked Serge for sharing this fragment about my grandfather—but even the dead-eye swallow tells the story over and over in its swoop and dive. The third question: what is about to return?

At Sardent (II)

If a story satisfies, it has the power to hinder, and if it hinders then it has the power to satisfy.

One of my great-uncles married a Catholic woman. Her name was Jeanne. When the invaders approached, the family fled Paris for the hiding places acquired in her name. Thirty-seven people.

Within each story is a substance, saline and tidal, wearing down the shape of the telling.

Upon arriving at the dirt road alongside the fields where my mother once dug potatoes in her school shoes, Cousin Genevieve, uncertain which farmhouse had been hers, nearly fainted. From the heat, she said.

Something about a story is antagonistic, saying there is a coming that never stops, eventually you'll have to sleep but I'll keep spilling, spreading beneath your bed.

Finally Genevieve said yes, this is the house. Rented by summer people from Neuilly-sur-Seine. With their permission, my daughters walked through the grounds.

If a story swirls around its own desire, then it neither satisfies nor hinders. No halting from breathlessness or frustration. Neither plunders nor escapes.

We looked across the vast field. But in case of emergency, our parents told us to run into those woods behind the house, Genevieve said. May I have a drink of water, she asked the renters.

When the family returned to Paris, their possessions were gone.

The path after it has been traveled from end to end—I look back despite the hazards. As if presences here lack something vital. The depletion is the peril.

One of my friends has been gripped by *petites morts* since she was a child. Each time, she doesn't know if she will return.

For your mother, there was no return, Genevieve said. Something else had arrived during her absence from Paris. It blocked the way.

A Detail from "At Sardent (II)"

At last Genevieve said yes, this is the house,
but the outbuildings are gone, the barn and sheds.
Across the dirt road, cornstalks filled the field,
a month from harvest. She was squinting
at the unrustling crop as if a moment
of danger had arrived. Very strange, she said,
the French don't eat corn, we would feed it
to the geese, what little we grew back then.
Ah but today we are the world's third largest
exporter of corn said the man who lives
in the house. You are looking at enough polenta
to feed the popes for eternity.

An Argument in the Street

I walked straight toward the shouting and passed by the market on the Rue de Seine, a shopping list in my hand.

The two were arguing on the sidewalk, the woman striding away, then stopping to turn back and abuse the man who in turn would halt a few steps behind her. I understood quickly that she had bought some tulips in the flower shop and he, a clerk there, had followed her out of the shop where some part of the transaction had gone awry.

Yes, she had ordered some irises as well, but he had sold the last of the white ones she preferred.

The desire to please—suppose there is a child who can do nothing to assuage the fear and despondency of the mother. Trying to gratify her diminishes, hour by hour, the chance for something. What is it?

Now the space between the woman and man was growing, her paces were of a uniform length but his steps were losing intention. Under the repeated punishments of her remarks, he became calmer. He looked up at the sky or maybe at a high window.

Scribbled on the other side of my list—turning back to the market, neither to search the streets and help complete her arrangement nor to buy some flowers in the man's shop to restore his benign routine of commerce. Mid-day hour of acts undone. Radishes, shallots, lemons, lettuce.

Transit

Everything is on time
which entails waiting for what is due
which expends time as if everything is late

The commuter train won't cross the state line,
it stops short of trespass like a mortal in a myth
who passes up a concierge tour of Hades

My mother says once again "I don't know how
we managed to escape Paris, your grandmother pulled me
up into the train, she was shrieking"

I drove my daughter to the station, I carried
one of her bags to the platform, between the station
and the platform there's a walkway

The tracks that carried me to this moment
have melted and seeped away, still their vibrations
resonate to the deepest underworld

My daughter's train departed on time,
puncturing state borders to the south at speeds
resulting in an aura of almost early arrival

I remained on the walkway, gazing down
the narrowing space between station and tracks,
milkweed, chunks of tar, dirt and disuse

Father returned from work to find mother
in bed *très désespéré*. Why? the boy asked, the kind
of question that exposes its throat

Appalling powers may sweep in
and bear down without even wanting to
but now are sated and serene until the next train, on time

After a Sudden Death

Although we arrived promptly at the sanctuary, all the seats were taken except for those reserved for the mourning family who had not yet proceeded in solemnly, arms supporting each other. I paused at the rear entrance, looking up the center aisle at the casket.

An usher touched my arm and directed us to an overflow room, nearly empty. We sat in the second row before a large video screen—the camera, located in the sanctuary's balcony, stared down at the first few rows, the stage, speaker stands, and the casket.

Sitting in front of us was a woman with broad shoulders and a sun-burned neck. Her ears were also severely irritated. When she brushed her hand against her left earlobe, a crystal pendant fell to the floor. I bent to retrieve it but had to get down on my knees to reach the jewel under her chair. When I rose, she also stood and thrust out her hand. I gazed into her extended palm for what seemed like a long time. It was very quiet, there was no sound coming from the video speakers.

Then some motion broke my reverie—on the screen, the people rose from their seats. My friend, whose wife had died suddenly three days earlier, came into the sanctuary with his family. After they were shown to their seats, an officiate appeared to begin his address but we couldn't hear.

Someone rushed out of our room to alert the funeral manager to the audio malfunction. I thought, there is no word for what is now happening. Now my friend's two children arranged themselves around him, the boy leaning in at his side, the girl shifting onto her father's lap. I thought, there is a lost sound in this lamentation, not obliging anyone to respond. A sound spoken to no one but the thing that matches the poverty of my powers to move or speak.

The woman and I were still standing, facing each other. It seemed like a long time, maybe the others were watching us. Then my palm opened.

No-Show

When there are more chairs than people,
there's no way to count those unattending.
They move about in the streets all the way down
to the interstate, or disperse into the suburbs.

No point in the tally of empty seats
but the house manager counts them anyway.

Some no-shows believe nothing has ever begun,
others say everything ends too soon
or goes on too long. Some arrive but hang around
the cash bar and leave before the start.

Putting people in chairs
used to be my job, I was so adept at capacity
the fire marshal had me on his do-not-trust list
but would stay for the show.

How people leaned
against the walls of the gathering place,
each original or copied posture.

But now, chairs willing to take the brunt
go unweighted, the room and everything in it
seem less momentous. The uncountable missing
give one-to-five stars to other affairs.

You come here, you get pegged
as a no-show in untold places,
as preferring aftermaths to events.

But this is where time and space sacrifice themselves
to walk-in music and opening remarks.

Not the refreshments table this time
but a piece of pastry fallen beside it.
Not the stack of program booklets
but the barstool on which they're placed.

And windblown snow ticking
against the big mullioned windows.

Creaking, the sparse audience shifts in their seats—
spaces deepening to accommodate the ones
out of range.

Anniversary

Soon the wedding party will emerge from the cathedral,
the brass doors will swing open on blackened hinges.
A small crowd gathers in the piazza, twenty, thirty people.

About our wedding, my wife has said many times,
"I wasn't sure until the last moment if he'd show up."
Blithe story, its repetition amasses a man
forever on the verge of vanishing.

Minibuses and cars line up to transport
the celebrants to a dinner in the country.
No trace on the cobblestones of this morning's rain.

At a table on the edge of the piazza, my wife tastes
chocolate mousse gelato from my spoon.
The clown of Perugia, striped pants and floppy green hat,
introduces himself with a bow below the church steps,
a few children gather around, more people stop to watch.

On my tongue the flavor of her cappuccino gelato
has almost disappeared. The fading precedes
everything the tongue will say and the eye will want.

The clown says, Here, little girl, from balloons I have made
a hat for you, an orange hare atop a blue halo, and for you, little boy,
can you guess what shape this is?

The doors will open, the people will applaud,
the drivers will start the engines.

Deep within the cathedral, locked inside a nest
of fifteen boxes, is the Holy Wedding Ring of the Virgin,
each box matched to a different key,
each key etched with her name.

"The Utrillo Is Lost Forever"

Sascha entrusted the painting to a colleague at *Vogue Paris*. In 1939 at age eighteen, she had been hired as an illustrator. When she and our family returned from Sardent after hiding from the Germans and the Vichy for five years, the painting was gone.

Utrillo had given it to her just before the war. By then he was too infirm to paint *en plein air*, he would gaze out his windows and paint what he saw or create from postcards or photographs of Paris streets. He had given up drinking, become religious, and married.

Sascha's lost Utrillo was a painting of the triangular five-story building where Erik Satie had lived in Arcueil. There have been rumors of the artwork's appearance in Rublyovka and Abu Dhabi. Wherever there are billionaires, there is art. A disgruntled servant, blackmail, collapse of an estate due to a sudden change of fortune—news of missing art gets out.

Utrillo's mother was Suzanne Valadon, a model in great demand, then a painter. Maybe Renoir or Degas was Utrillo's father. "To have this succession of lovers was madness itself," she wrote in her memoir. She made a famous painting of Satie in 1892 when she was twenty-seven years old.

I went to Paris for the first time in 1966 and stayed with Sascha in Auteuil for a month, then we took the train to Locarno on my sixteenth birthday. She was my mother's first cousin, twenty-nine years older than I. She had lustrous dark hair, a beauty mark beside her chin, smoked with a cigarette holder, spoke with the family's Russo-French accent but with a slight lisp, and liked to spend mornings in her long robe drinking coffee and sketching. There is a pen and ink drawing of me reading a newspaper.

Sascha mentioned the Utrillo many times—without rancor for the colleague at *Vogue* who had no explanation for the painting's disappearance. It had been taken to his family's house in Brittany, and one could not have envisioned the fighting and destruction that occurred there in 1944.

About her pregnancy, Suzanne Valadon recalled her friend Adele saying, "He should have used a goatskin on his cock." The boy grew up with seizures, was often beaten by her lovers, and became a drunk by age eighteen.

Sascha took me to see Satie's building. To this day, my cousins enjoy teasing me. They ask, "Where else did she take you? What else did you learn about art?"

House Falling into the Sea

Two houses are in peril, one atop a cliff,
the other a hundred and twenty feet below.

Many opinions are proposed on what should be done
to keep the sea from sweeping them away.

The first house, atilt on the edge of the head,
looks like a shipwreck hauled up from the sea and hung to dry.

The other, below, quivers on piles.
Look up, tumbling clay and stones are heard

before they are seen, then thud and roll onto the beach.
At low tide, bulldozers and bucket loaders

dump sand at the high tide mark.
Up on the cliff, a view of seawater streaked with masses of sand

drifting away to new bars and beaches down the coast.
Look below, layers of stone set into the slope,

a revetment against the wind, the overwash.
A cameraman shoots the sunlit façade, up from the base.

If you ever fall down a cliff,
lean back so you don't topple forward,

that's the engineer's advice. A plan to move the house
away from the plunge. Arguments against.

Below, two men shoulder a rolled rug
from the house on stilts. Then, a mattress.

A few grains of sand detach from each other,
something slips imperceptibly. Then, a painting of a yacht.

II.

Aground

The paths pinched off, the ventures
I prepared for but did not pursue—students
learned from others, jobs were filled by others,
trains departed without me, I prised hooks from fish
because none were the elusive bass.

We told stories that evening, old friends of former lives
getting reacquainted with the gaps
between us. Many recollections, with whiskey breath,
of all the lettings-go. Then to bed.

In the morning there was news,
the radio tuned to the local station—
Miss Renata, a 49-foot conch boat, had run aground
on Lobsterville Beach while we slept, the captain slumped
at the wheel, his mate drunk below deck. Nobody here eats conch.
Today they would have unloaded their haul in New Bedford
for processing, then the frozen whelk would have steamed to Quanzhou.

None of us on the ridge above the beach
woke to the air klaxon of the Coast Guard, multiple hails
that failed to rouse the captain. We were dreaming.
The usual route of the *Miss Renata*—the captain, knowing the currents,
distances and shoals—was he oppressed by his certainties?
The beer bottles clanked as the ship rolled.
He cut himself off from his destination.

That afternoon I went to the dump
where the talk was about irresponsibility, folly.
They towed the vessel to the harbor, then revoked
the captain's docking privileges. He told the *Gazette*,
"To be honest, it's pretty embarrassing." At that moment

how could he entrust himself to anything? The sounds
resonated for everyone but him—the scrape of the keel
on the stony bottom, the shouts of those trying to make things right,
make an arrest, make the foolish pay
for the exertion of the law at 4 a.m.

The Dangers of Contemplation

Follow the seagull aloft
in arcs above the ballpark.
The mind can go that high and far.

The mind can hover surreptitiously
staring into the open skull of the stadium
and pick out something small resting there
and call it the enigma

in miniature. Popcorn kernel. Bottle cap.
Or a scattering of peanut shells.
So many spectators stained with condiments,
singing *for spacious skies* believing we see more
than the gull can see.

Inevitably, one of two things occurs:
A. Vertigo as you look down
on the gull drifting like a dust mote miles below.
Or even worse, B. Confusion everlasting.

A baseball manager once said:
If you make a pitcher do something
they don't want to do, no telling
how their arm will react.
The inner life, sealed.
The outer life, concealed.

The smell of the breath of the gull
is swirling above the pitcher's mound.
The soul is the breath? The cry?

Then, the soul is what tumbles
from the gull's anus onto a windshield
in the parking lot just as a broken-bat single
plops into short left.

The mind can go this far.
The ace's arm aspires to infinite angles
but three good pitches are sufficient.

Six relievers smell adversity in their pen.
The gull flies blindly in our sleep.
The spiritual life must not go too deep.

Naked City

He was apprehended in Herald Square carrying the head of his sister-in-law
by her sprung hair. Hoop earrings. He said, *I'm trapped in a story I heard.*
Unsure of motive, the DA couldn't say where the accused,
striding through the streets, was going.

*

On victory night, when celebrations erupt,
young men rock a pizza delivery van, striving for something
unprecedented but find no means, no proper subject.
Meanwhile, a videographer shooting a blocked intersection,
violence in her viewfinder, makes
no remark, here where photographers wearing fedoras
once belittled the corpses with tart epithets:

A Bottom-Feeder was one who plummeted into a river from a bridge.
A Roast was the shape carried from a blaze.
A man lying in the street after a hit-and-run was a Flat Mammal.
A Dry Diver leapt from a ledge into the street.

Against the density of darkness, grotesque angle of neck to torso,
the flashgun's light was so intrusive and swift
the police were printed in odd, feckless positions
as if they'd relinquished control of their bodies.

*

Even after decades of seeing these things
explicated with captions of gangland hits and strangled hookers,
the city still gave rise to libidinous visions, couplings
on rooftop gardens, giddy spillage in limousines—

while in the street below streaming headlines
across the façades of commerce, the transaction
between newspaper vendor and customer was wordless.
The dire images and descriptions exchanged hands.

*

We were walking up Broadway—a cab swerved
to avoid another cab and jumped the curb, harming no one,
but knocked in the side of a newspaper stall and startled the seller within.
A man took his child in his arms, *we've been saved*
he said as a page of newsprint shrouded his feet.

*

Zoom in on a cop's son crushed under the overturned pizza van.
Everyone move back, move back, move back!

*

A city is coming,
not the city of the future or the world to come,
but the city of our glimpse and tread.
A city that may not ever be our city.
So proclaims a soiled evangelist with a sign
misspelled with sins as crowds leave
the stadium after a season-ending win.
High spirits, someone tosses him a bag of nuts.

*

A few inches in today's paper:
An ancient river has been found, not in our city
but beneath Toronto. A cap blew off an artesian well.
While workers repaired it, another top blew nearby—
the Laurentian River, long surmised
in a soaking valley of bedrock debris,
had exposed itself at last.

Hydrologists could only speak of it, there are no images.
The water is drinkable, with a ferrous tang.
Sitting on a park bench, a young woman reads this story
on her news feed, then says aloud to no one
it's time to repair the broken fountains filled with leaves.

Ask Me Now

The towering Norway spruces set out in a row to break the north winds—
there is no way to speak for them. The fragmented stories
of their violent struggles are lost in the tales of the great storms.

But when the blizzard attains its full force, that's the moment to search
for the teaspoon lost during the lawn party last summer—
there it is, with everything else revealed to be buried.

I packed up my mother's belongings and sold her house.
Embroidered with birds, tablecloth stained and torn—
always both altar cloth and shroud.

A memory is a fever of phrases, my answer will falter
if you ask me now about the wounded bat that flew
to my pillow, or the striped bass reeled in from shore during a hurricane,

or the thump of the neighbor's dog under the Chrysler's left rear tire.
Whatever preceded or followed after those creatures is lost,
what persists is where things paused. Ask me anyway.

Handbags wrapped in tissue, hammered copper pans
brought back from France, a stack of big band CDs—
as with sandbags tethering the balloon to earth

someone has to undo the knots. Dull edge of a carving knife,
border of wallpaper remnant, narrowing neck of a cruet—
an end discovered everywhere.

From a Line by Kawabata

A solitary shadow in stillness
hoping for snow.

She stands with an invoice in her pocket
for services rendered poorly.

Are there two winds? There's a ceiling of cloud
sliding slowly, and cirrus rushing elsewhere.

The day seems unsuited for business,
settling accounts. Yet it hints of results.

Just a moment ago
was a thousand years of insufficiency.

Now, there's a scenic plenitude,
and the ache in her temples is passing.

Determined not to pay, she resents
the displeasure that ruins a day.

The pine needle is an emblem
of a thousand-year-old scene:

the Enlightened Beggar pointing
at the substance of hoped-for things—

the crystalline scent of a cloud
about to relinquish its load.

The land will gain something infinite.
The sky will be freed of something infinite.

This landscape, so capable
of carrying what the sky delivers!

Then she asks: Why should I accept
the faulty work of this man?

Surely the snow is arriving,
piled deeply above, everything in balance.

But it's no good. Such a foolish idea,
this perfect settling of snow.

One must deal with dissatisfaction,
and also, the clouds are breaking up,

the pallid-blue sky pushes through
and a flake of moon says *you must pay.*

At a Conference on the Syrian Exiles

While he spoke for the special case of exiles, our shoes sent roots into the floorboards.

Responding to a question, he shouted from the podium—*So you feel like an exile from the life you think you deserve! So you think everyone is banished by the mere passage of time! But you are no refugee!*

He appeared to be glaring out beyond the back row of the audience where someone was hurrying out, perhaps to use the restroom or to catch a flight.

I remember, coming home from the grassy lot where we played ball— with fearful anger my mother asked, "Do you think any of your friends would move a finger to save your life?" Yet she had been saved by people who were not even friends, hidden in a hay cellar under the floor of a stable.

Further shouting from the dais—*Don't tell me we are all stateless, don't tell me I am imagining things such as countries and their executioners!*

I remember, on the day a New York shuttle plane fell into Boston Harbor, wrecked by a flock of starlings, I walked to Quincy Square to watch the trains come and go. She sent the police to find me.

Now the speaker was addressing us Americans—*You know, the world once counted on you for justice. When the French occupied Syria, your President Wilson's commission trekked to 300 villages between Manbij and Beersheba, and talked with the people, and angered the League of Nations by proclaiming the people should rule themselves.*

What if I claim the savagery crouched at the outset of my life? You are right to ask which savagery.

My mother's contorted cursive on the signature line of a Do Not Resuscitate form.

A man never to return to Aleppo asks for a drink of water before he passes out. The person answering his plea is the one running from the lecture hall.

Neighborhood Watch

Peer at things, look closely at the row of cedars
in their scented innocence warmed by the sun.

The bushes mark the boundary
between organizations of habit and means,
the street running alongside all units
converts with one click to an emergency route.

Open the window, the impact of footsteps
on the sidewalk sends a wave through the earth
all the way to a folk music festival in Budapest.

Behold the walker, then look right through him—
can you see the Hungarian girls in embroidered dresses
dancing in a circle to an ocarina and drum?

The sound of cedars drinking what they can
is all one hears in the space between the walker
and the girls. The walker is a teenager—
he would be captivated by Hungarian boys
doing the ancient bootslap dance.

The streetlamps flicker on, the walking boy
casts a shadow and his body gains density.
When he stops on the sidewalk to peer through the dusk,
regard him and say this to the cedars: *I fear I am only
a shadow and I am afraid of shadows.*
Lower your weapon and look.

Between the Bed and the Window

First, the light, which is always
perfect if it's arriving
from the sky, at this moment
indirectly from the east,
reflected off the banked clouds
in the window and making
the dim bedroom visible
including my feet, having
followed the familiar arc
from under the wool blanket
to oak floor, so each morning
the initial view faces
toward the north, just as it was
when I was a child, northward
to Boston with silvery
propjets descending over
my town of gray granite steps.
The light which lets one abide,
noticing the small details
such as the plastic vial
of pills knocked off the nightstand
and the novel beside it
on the floor, the dustcover
with its drawing of faces,
the bookmark fallen from place.
And just as you can get lost
among imaginary
people living in Peru,
you may risk losing your hold
on the world when bearing down
faithfully on the objects
between the bed and window,

in fact you may disappear,
like the child who wandered far
all the way to the shipyard
and stood by the great gateway
as the early morning shift
passed through to Old Colony
Avenue and the late shift
entered. A waking presence
makes a transit between warmth
of sleep and sounds in the street.
Between the bed and window
he notices the fine dust
on the sill. He isn't there.

Stop-Time

Frank McCabe bought on credit at my father's liquor store,
they had gone to school together. Finally my father said,
teach my son to play drums and we're even, for now.

Late afternoon lessons in his cellar, first the basics
rapped out on rubber pads, then rolls, drags, flams, paradiddles and
    ratamacues.
Moving on to a real kit and the flair of fills, underbelly routines
of the bass and flights between cymbals, sizzle and crash.

While I practiced, he scribbled on charts for his quintet—
Thursdays at the Knotty Pine and weddings on weekends.
No lessons for most of the summer after his heart attack.

Autumn rain, water seeping up between linoleum tiles,
staining the peeling baseboards. Mold and mildew,
backbeat and double time. Smoker's cough and drinker's nose.
Soon he set up his kit next to mine, laying out the opening bars
of "From This Moment On" and I'd play inside him.
That's how he put it, stay inside me and listen with your wrists.

When Mrs. McCabe came down to say they caught the man
who killed the president, he dropped the needle on "Opus One"
and said play. We listened to Krupa's "Rockin' Chair"
and Buddy Rich's big band doing "Time Check."

Lying on their sides, quarts of bourbon behind cans
of dried paint. You don't wiggle, pivot or rock your feet
on the pedals, speed comes from control. You don't keep time,
you make time. The standards, renowned yet open to reinvention,
thus eternal. But I lived inside a body, Mrs. McCabe returned

from the hospital with no breasts, a week later
she was playing piano upstairs while Frank critiqued—

Don't play with your whole arm, it looks cool
but it isn't. He lit a Winston. Don't be like a bass player,
use deodorant. Never let a wimp carry your gear.
Listen carefully to the songs you hate the most.

Verse and chorus, shuffle, bridge, fill, drag, fill, stop-time,
ghost-note. Rumble of the sagging boiler, steam knocking the pipes.
Soon you won't have to remember, you'll just make the sound.

"What Is This Thing Called Love?"

My mother said go get me a plum.
When I got to the fridge, she said
and some almonds.

In the cabinet, the airtight calm
of a canned baby ham.

My grandmother lost a forefinger
while slicing onions! No you silly,
she got an infection. The headache
unsteadied her hand, the knife slipped.
A tumor in her skull the size of an onion.

Thirteen years old, we were shooting
straight pool at the bowladrome.
The eight ball lived a separate life,
Joey and Mark said no matter what
they won't obey Father Byrne anymore.

Go get me a cigarette, she said,
and some chocolate.

Joey said, Yeah, I'll tell you what it tastes like.
It tastes like my mother's pork leftovers
rotting in the garbage for a week.

The radio said there was an earthquake
but I didn't feel it. Put Ella Fitzgerald
on the stereo, she said.

The catalpa must have died that fall,
or over the winter, or just an hour ago,

or a second. They ground up the stump,
planted a spindly dogwood.

I lay in bed, transistor under my pillow,
the countdown to number one. Joey told us
it's really a song about sex. The radio said
the earthquake was a 3.8. I could hear
my mother and father making plans
on the other side of the wall.

Next morning, the radio said
there had been an after-tremor.
I was sure it was a song about speeding
far away with a girl.

Dog Pacing a Balcony

On a balcony six floors up,
a brown dog paces. Four or five steps,
a sharp turn, then repeats.

The dog is observed through a window
in the building opposite, across a concrete plaza.
The watchers, diabetics awaiting treatment,
are also six floors up.

Every so often, someone looks up from a magazine
or out of a reverie and squints at the dog.
A name is called out, a patient rises for examination,
and another arrives. How long will it take her
to discover the dog?

There are side effects no one has documented,
you look at something and your blood's sweetness
could feed a hummingbird or enrage a hawk.
The latter, red-tailed, swoops by the window.

It isn't sickness—the lonely frenzy of the dog
is making the watchers a little lightheaded.
A nurse offers half cups of orange juice.

I accompany my mother to her appointment,
the dog is visible over the doctor's shoulder.
As the thunderstorm begins, the space
between us and the dog is impenetrable.

At the checkout desk, one final glance—
the dog's frantic march is finished.
It laps up the rain in its dish.

Image of a Path Through Woods

October, the first fallen
leaves cover the trail through woods,
it's noon, the sun already
tilting away towards winter
but the canopy persists
and lights up in bright patches.
This is where a person stopped.
Eyes gazing down the umbral
lane streaked with diluted glow.
Then the shutter admitted
the slanted light. You can see—
just below frame's center,
that's where the path comes to end
in a smudge of sunlight. This
is where a person perceived
a destination, a fate,
a proposition, a trap.
The image marshals the mind
to autobiography
as if there is no peril
when a person turns their back
on what isn't visible.
The path compels one to plan
but the underbrush says *don't*.
This is where a person stood
still, where we notice the leaves
in foreground are in focus,
the fallen bough lying there.
The end of the path is blurred.
Everything in us derives
from something else, someone else
dreamed up this myth of the path.

The image is inspiring
and gives us hope to go on—
that's the thought that marks the way,
mars the way with desperate
knowledge of how to proceed.
It was my cousin Camille,
a painter, who said *Our art
gets in the way of looking
so we might envision what's
invisible.* The trail bikes
are approaching from behind.
Step aside, they don't intend
to stop. And they will perform
the essential act—throwing
their slashing shadows against
the unwavering image.

Recessional

Traveling to enter the enriching distances,
the names of places like a sequence of songs—
in a single night the charm was broken.

Sliding two more inches to the east,
the Andes put themselves just out of reach.

Receding, now even the next room is as remote
as the village in Ghana where they crown a stranger
king for a day and wrap them in woven garments.

From dawn horizon to the other quick to darken,
soon it appears the world is simply binary.

The hairbrush forgotten at the bathroom sink—
in one voice the bristles call across the sea
surely you see how things fall away!

A passport stamp isn't an approval,
it says you may proceed but your desire
is vaporous as a contrail and not a winged cylinder.

Once, after clearing customs in Narita Airport,
I collapsed, and when my eyes opened
yet another outset was announced
through the boisterous terminal.

The world appears binary but it's a choppy flight
from pole to pole, the imagination so capable
it feeds off stale air and salty snacks.

In my time I was flung like a baited hook
from a tree limb extended over the waters,

and when the stars blinked in the gastric eye of the shark—
that was the city of Copenhagen.

Boat Too Costly to Keep

Weeks of studying Portuguese
while my father lay dying in the hospice bed.

Final hour, his inhalations deepened
like those of a man rowing.

We buried him, and three days later I drove
to the broad canal maybe to catch a bass among the Brazilians.

Wednesday morning, three men, close in age,
casting off the rocky bank. Then, one of them shouting—

in the middle of the canal, a boat drifted by,
a motor yacht, unrigged, a shackle clanging on the mainsail mast.

No one aboard, no one would huddle in the cabin,
borne away like that, unless they were demented.

Carried down the current, north to south.
The men looked on silently, checking bait and recasting.

The boat was slowly turning, starboard side
facing the current, then turned to float backwards,

then spun around abeam to port,
then to drift as before—

so far beyond everyone now,
a strain to watch the stern disappear.

Now the men were laughing
because an abandoned boat, so diminished

in value, so expensive to moor and maintain
and so loaded with debt,

had been christened with such a name.
It was a joke and I understood every word.

Joy Ride

All the way down the street events occur
from which I'm held back, but in response to this blockage
their sounds and smells draw closer. An insult shouted from a passing car.
A burst of music and voices when the weathered door of the Knotty Pine
opens and two young women emerge, they came out from the tavern
and paused on the sidewalk beside a black-and-white idling at the curb,
the two cops had disappeared around the corner to lift a trash bin
tipped into the gutter as a prank, and the women scrambled
into the police car and sped away down Hancock Street.

But between the opening of the door of the Knotty Pine
and the screech of tires, the women's eyes swept over mine,
one hand gestured, and I got into the front seat with them.
There was the precipice, then the fall and tumble
flattening out into flight that in the span of my life
has never touched down, though when she who was driving,
she with the blue raincoat and clacking bracelet, said *at the L Street bathhouse
you're getting out, whoever you are*, I did. Some minutes later
they were stopped by the Boston police as the *Globe* later reported
in the copy I bought from the box outside the Knotty Pine

and the apartment I rented above with the slanted floor,
a view of a row of stores across the street, now eight stories
of condos, from the higher floors you can see the bay
and the boulevard we raced down towards the city
listening to the dispatcher telling us to stop before things go
too far, *how far is that?* the other one beside me asked,
she with the ponytail lighting up one of the cops' Marlboros,
her exhalations in my lungs, as years later on business flights
over oceans I inhaled everything depleted
and watched a film in which an anthropologist, having observed apes
attack their ape adversaries, still insisted humans are worth developing

even as some massacre or other was happening miles below
the refreshment cart coming haltingly down the aisle,
which makes me recall that the cops had also left behind, what else?
a bag of glazed doughnuts with which we took communion,
the rite of passage to another body by absorption, and truly
I've been so many persons and have carried them with me
from the beginning like some winged transport, de-iced
every morning and feeling upon waking as if someone
had been driving my car all night and tossed her trash
into the back seat while in dreams I eluded my enemies.

What has been withheld is fated to take form, the ancient laurel trees
are finally visible, all the way to Madeira I went to witness them
and the footpaths and irrigation channels, a craving for the memory
in the bodies of the landscape—the young women turned
into laurel trees, so the myth goes, in order to hide from Apollo—
a craving for anything that lasts longer than a few minutes of escape
which nevertheless are pitched against the years of dubious salaried effort
that demanded all my artifice and the emphatic movement of my hands
making a convincing case for what would master and dispose of me.
Office clothes I no longer wear, stuffed in a black plastic bag and shoved
into the Goodwill Industries receptacle, specifically the one
two blocks down from the Knotty Pine which took forty-five minutes
to get to, all the way with two remorseless young women
embodied in a radio song sung to whomever I am.

Notes

"At Sardent" / Sardent is a village in the Creuse department in France, population 779 (2018). During World War II, it was under the jurisdiction of the Vichy.

"He Decided to Go to Kuzguncuk" / Kuzguncuk is an Istanbul neighborhood in the Üsküdar district on the Asian side of the Bosphorus.

"The Utrillo is Lost Forever" / Maurice Utrillo (1883-1955) was a French painter noted for his Paris cityscapes.

"The Dangers of Contemplation" / Based on a warning in the Kabbalah. The poem's last line is quoted from *Branch Rickey's Little Blue Book* (Macmillan 1995).

"From a Line by Kawabata" / The quoted line is from Yasunari Kawabata's story "Nature" (1958), translated by Michael Emmerich.

"Neighborhood Watch" / In memory of Trayvon Martin (1995-2012).

"Stop-Time" / Stop-time is a jazz gesture in which the drummer plays a few notes of the rhythm with especially sharp accents.

"What is This Thing Called Love" / The title of one of Ella Fitzgerald's signature hit songs, written by Cole Porter.

"Image of a Path Through Woods" / Inspired by a photograph by Scott Crawford.